A Preparatory Foundation for Pastoral Ministry

Ministerial Apprentice Program (MAP)

Maynard H. Belt

FORWARD

"A wise man will hear, and will increase learning; and a man of understanding shall attain unto wise counsels." Proverbs 1:5. *Maynard Belt has provided an exceptional source of "wise counsel" for pastoral ministry. It is an excellent discipleship manual for seasoned pastors to use in mentoring young men heading into ministry and it is a fine resource for all those presently in ministry as well.*

This outstanding handbook draws from many years of successful pastoral and ministry leadership roles. The product which you now have is a treasure trove of wisdom. His valuable insights and wisdom leap from every page of this concise manual. There is a richness of experience and Spirit-filled passion built into each lesson.

Maynard addresses key issues for pastoral ministry and gives priceless advice designed to prevent pastoral tragedies and build successful ministries. This manual meets a critical need for our day when there are troubling trends in shallow ministries and a growing dearth of pastoral prospects. Every wise pastor and prospective pastor will grow wiser by studying this excellent resource!

Kenneth J. Spink, Pastor
Berea Baptist Church, Berea, OH

There is nothing quite as valuable as the voice of experience. Such is the case in this rich collection of ministry wisdom from the life of one who has been tested and proven. Maynard Belt is one of the most gracious and genuinely godly slaves of the Lord I have been privileged to know and with whom I have served. The collection of topics in A Preparatory Foundation for Pastoral Ministry *accurately provides what its title states. It is a great preparation. It is a solid foundation. It is a comprehensive address of pastoral ministry.*

I am honored to recommend this practical study, generously supported with Scripture and promoting a worthy philosophy of ministry. Today's pastors and pastoral students will be greatly benefited as they engage in this helpful work. What a gift to the building of the Church!

Daniel L. Anderson, Th. D.
President, Appalachian Bible College

I recall sitting in Bible College and seminary classes observing a common scene. On the desk or podium at the front of each classroom was a worn manila folder. In the folder was a remarkable collection of outlines and notes from which the teacher taught the class. That collection of notes represented to me the extraordinary study, experience, and insight of the professor. I longed to achieve that level of knowledge, not just to pass a test, but to grasp the subject material and someday master the craft like the teacher.

When I first read the material contained in this study, I had a similar sense. I have known and observed Maynard for many years. I know him to have the heart and skill of a pastor. He has not only pastored churches but mentored pastors in ministry, helping them hone the skills of their trade.

Maynard's approach has always been to do ministry not merely with the latest trend but with a Biblical basis. You will find in these outlines and notes a timeless treasure of pastoral wisdom. I told Maynard, that I wish young men heading toward ministry today could have access to this foundational knowledge upon which they might build enduring ministries. Thank you, Maynard, for allowing us to look inside your manila folder. We'll be better pastors.

John Greening
National Representative
General Association of Regular Baptist Churches

This program, and its author, were integral in the realization of God's call on my life as well as my preparation into ministry! MAP has not only played a part in my life before ministry, but even now as I serve the Lord as a Youth Pastor I have been able to walk young men through this program, so they can see God's calling on their lives! The material found within these pages is Bible driven and written from years of pastoral experience. MAP is an amazing tool in the hand of a pastor looking to arm the next generation of pastors for the task that God has called us to!

Wes Crawford, Youth Pastor
MAP Graduate

Introduction

It has been a half century and a decade since the Lord delivered me as a teenager out of spiritual darkness and into His marvelous light, amazing grace and daily mercies. Reared in an unchurched home I came to faith on ground zero. There was much work that the Spirit of God had to do in my life. Within a few short months He brought me to that place where I bended to His will and said, *"Here's my life, Lord, no arguments!"* That decision directed me away from a secular university to a small Bible College simply to learn more about Him. This divinely directed path eventually led me into pastoral ministry and I began serving my first church at twenty-four years of age. I have had the privilege of pastoring four churches and sixteen years as representative of a fellowship of churches. My experiences with pastors and churches have been innumerable, many a blessing but also several very tragic. My particular academic training did not equip me for the practical aspects of serving as a pastor. It seemed that most of what I did was through trial and error and observance of other pastors I had come to know.

Thus, this endeavor concerning a preparatory foundation for pastoral ministry. First, it is very important to have a conviction regarding the call of God. I have known several who have missed the boat on this one. Next, it is important to know what ministry involves; and finally, whether one may be gifted for vocational ministry. My two-fold purpose is to give young men a preliminary view of pastoral ministry from a practical perspective, and to provide a resource for pastors/missionaries to use in mentoring such young men. It is a tool to use in continuing the discipleship process in the lives of those sensing the call into ministry. One young high school student having gone through this Ministerial Apprentice Program found it extremely helpful as he went off to Bible College and now, as a youth pastor, is using it to mentor some of his teens.

I have asked several pastor/missionary/educator friends for their evaluation and the response has been very positive. I recognize that some of the lessons are rather lengthy in content and may need more than one session to complete. I would want the instructor to follow the Lord's leading, as well as share his own experiences along life's journey. What I have shared has been mine. When teachable moments arise to the occasion, do not hesitate to take the time to pursue. Though not included here, I also gave students appropriate articles on the subject and sometimes books to add to their library.

I have been richly blessed to serve the Lord all of these years. It certainly has not always been a bed of roses but it has been an ever-increasing joy to know Him and the power of His resurrection, and the fellowship of His sufferings, and the honor of being conformed into His image. I would exhort pastors and missionaries everywhere to seek out those whom the Lord might be calling into ministry; pour your lives into them; and then send them out into the fields which remain white unto harvest.

Thankful for His grace,

Maynard H. Belt
Luke 9:62
mhbelt@sbcglobal.net
www.barnabasfile.com

A Preparatory Foundation for Pastoral Ministry
Maynard H. Belt

The purpose of this course is to give ministerial students a preliminary view of pastoral ministry from a practical perspective. It will familiarize those sensing a call from God into ministry some helpful insights that are not always taught in present day seminary curricula. Ministry is people and the closer we can get to them, the more effective we will be in serving them spiritually. Pastors are servant leaders. Warren Wiersbe defines ministry this way: "Ministry takes place when divine resources meet human needs through loving channels to the glory of God." Hopefully the following course of study will be beneficial to any recognizing God's special call upon their lives for vocational ministry.

Ministerial Apprentice Program (MAP)

Table of Contents

Ministers Are Earthen Vessels
II Corinthians 3-4

Spiritual treasures in earthen vessels
God's plan to spread His Word,
Able ministers with plainness of speech
Proclaiming Christ to those who haven't heard.

His mercy we have for this ministry
So that we faint not in the task.
Our sufficiency is all of God
If only we pray and ask.

Our message is Christ Jesus the Lord,
Ourselves we do not preach.
We are but servants for Jesus' sake,
So that others we might reach.

To proclaim God's glory to others
Is to reveal His character in us,
His love, His compassion, His mercy,
His truth, His holiness, and justice.

These earthen vessels may suffer,
Like Paul, hard-pressed on every side,
Perplexed, down cast and afflicted,
From morn to evening tide.

Yet not distressed, distraught or forsaken,
Nor destroyed by the works of death,
Bearing in his body the Lord Jesus,
Glorifying Him til earth's last breath.

Spiritual treasures in earthen vessels,
Able ministers called to serve,
How blessed we are to be chosen,
An honor we do not deserve.
–M.H. Belt

Ministerial Apprentice Program
(MAP)
Orientation Session (explanation)

Welcome to the Ministerial Apprentice Program (MAP). The purpose of this course is to give young men interested in vocational ministry an opportunity to learn what is involved in such a call from God. The Apostle Paul himself admitted that he became a minister according to the gift of the grace of God given unto him by the effective working of His (God) power (Ephesians 3:7). By participating in this class you are entering into the very classroom of God. Your instructor will be God Himself through His Holy Word and the enlightening of the Holy Spirit. Your teacher will simply be a facilitator. You are here by divine appointment to help you discern whether or not you have been given the greatest call ever given among mankind, a call to be a voice for God and servant to the greatest of all servants, Jesus Christ.

A call into ministry will put you in the likes of Abraham, Moses, Elijah, Elisha, Jonah, Jeremiah, Isaiah, Paul, Peter, John, Augustine, Luther, Spurgeon, Moody and a relatively small unknown number of others compared to the large number of all mankind. If you are genuinely called, you cannot run - Jonah tried! If you are called you cannot say you cannot speak – Moses tried! If you are called you cannot die before your time – Elijah tried! If you are called you cannot say that you are too weak – God said to Paul, *"My grace is sufficient!"*

You may not know where God's call may take you, but you will never be alone (Heb. 13:5). You may be overwhelmed at times by the responsibilities before you but through prayer you will receive wisdom (James 1:5). You may be chosen to be a martyr for the Gospel's sake, but only because you have been chosen trustworthy by our eternal God (I Tim. 1:12). Puritan John Flavel said, *"When the will of Christ is understood and known, we have no liberty of choice, but we must be governed by it, even if the duty commanded is very difficult, or the sin forbidden very tempting."*

Following is the course of study to be taken. There may also be opportunities to attend a deacon council meeting, missions committee meeting, participate in visitation, sit on the floor in the nursery and maybe even teach Sunday School classes from pre-school through adults. Arm your soul with a life verse from

God's holy Word. Expect great temptations from the wicked one. Pray daily that you might know HIS will. Put into practice what you learn and *"Journal your journey!"*

1. Orientation Session
2. The Pastor and the Will of God
3. The Pastor and His Calling
4. The Pastor and His Prayer Life
5. The Pastor as Servant Leader
6. The Pastor and His Care Ministry
7. The Pastor's Leadership Qualities
8. The Pastor and Leadership Disciplines
9. The Pastor and His Ministry Schedule
10. The Pastor's Personal Accountability
11. The Pastor and His Preaching
12. The Pastor and His Preaching Calendar
13. The Pastor and Ministerial Transitions
14. A Pastor's Lessons Learned in Laboring for the Lord

The Pastor and the Will of God

Introduction:

A. Of all people you might expect a pastor to know what the will of God is for his life. Some things regarding the will of God are very clear: be born-again; obey the Lord in water baptism; become a member of the church; read the Word of God daily; pray; give; serve. These are givens. In fact every believer should follow the Lord in these very basic first steps following salvation. Having an assured knowledge that one has been called to Christ must always pre-empt a call to ministry.

B. We are called to be reflectors of the grace and glory of God. This journey begins with our call to Christ, continues with our call to mission in life, and culminates when we are ultimately conformed into the image of Christ.

C. God loves you and has a plan for your life. No doubt you have heard this many times. But it is true. This plan was foreordained before the foundation of the world, especially the call to ministry. It was for Jeremiah (Jeremiah 1:4-5). Therefore you must be found often at the throne room of grace and mercy (Hebrews 4:14-16) in order to discern God's particular will for you. Don't treat it lightly.

What is the ultimate known will of God?

1. Conformation – Romans 8:29.
2. Transformation – Romans 12:1-2.
3. Completion – Colossians 4:12b.
4. Sanctification – I Thessalonians 4:3a.
5. Glorification – Isaiah 43:7; Romans 8:30.

How can I discern His perfect will for my life?

1. Through the ministry of the Holy Spirit – John 14:26; 16:13.
2. Through His Word – Psalm 119:105.

3. Through Godly counsel – Proverbs 11:14; 15:22.
4. Through His peace – Philippians 4:7; Colossians 3:15.
5. Through His reproving love – Hebrews 12:6.

Has God given me any indication that He will help me find His will for my life?

1. His direction – Isaiah 30:20-21; Psalm 32:8; 37:23.
2. His wisdom – Colossians 1:9; James 1:5.
3. His working – Philippians 1:6; 2:13.
4. His presence – Isaiah 43:2; Hebrews 13:5.
5. His compassion – Isaiah 63:9.

What must I work on to stay within the will of God?

1. Remain obedient to His Word – Psalm 40:7-8; II Timothy 3:16-17.
2. Be willing daily to be a living sacrifice – Romans 12:1-2.
3. Walk always in His ways – Proverbs 4:25-27.
4. Be consistent in your prayer life – Jeremiah 29:11-13; Matthew 7:7-8.
5. Use your common sense – II Timothy 1:7.

An Acrostic to Evaluate a Call to Ministry

Confirmation: Has your church confirmed that God has called you (I Timothy 4:14)?

Abilities: do you have the necessary abilities to teach, shepherd and oversee the flock (I Timothy 3:2)?

Longing: Do you aspire to the office of overseer (I Timothy 3:1)?

Life: Is your character above reproach (I Timothy 3:2-7)?

James M. George, *The Call to Pastoral Ministry*

Thy way, not mine, O Lord, however dark it be!
Lead me by Thine own hand, Choose out the path for me.
Smooth let it be or rough, it will be still the best;

winding or straight, it leads right onward to Thy rest.
I dare not choose my lot; I would not, if I might; choose
Thou for me, my God; so shall I walk aright.
The kingdom that I seek is Thine; so let the way that leads to it be
Thine; else I must surely stray.
Take Thou my cup, and it with joy or sorrow fill, as best to
Thee may seem; choose Thou my good and ill.
Choose Thou for me my friends, my sickness or my health;
choose Thou my cares for me, my poverty or wealth.
Not mine, nor mine the choice, in things great or small; be
Thou my guide, my strength, my wisdom, and my all!
–Horatius Bonar

The Pastor and His Calling

Understanding the Call of God
Luke 9:1-10; 57-62

1. **Ministry begins with a call to vocation – Luke 9:1 (He called)**

   a) We have been divinely chosen by God the Father – Isa. 43:10; Amos 7:14-15.
   b) We have been divinely chosen by God the Son – I Tim. 1:12.
   c) We have been divinely chosen by God the Holy Spirit – Acts 20:28.
   d) We have been deemed faithful – I Tim. 1:12.
   e) We have been designed purposely – Eph. 3:7-8.

2. **God assures us of His provision – Luke 9:1 (He gave)**

   a) Whenever God calls He enables – especially in our helpless times – I Timothy 1:12.
   b) We can draw upon His wisdom through His Word; His strength in our weakness; Upon His grace and mercy in our need. James 1:5; II Cor. 12:9-10; Heb. 12:16.
   c) The Throne Room is always open – Heb. 4:14-16.

3. **God directs us to a location – Luke 9:2 (He sent)**

   a) Important to know that where we are is where God has placed us. Psalm 18:30.
   b) Should it ever be time to leave, He will guide us and lead us. Psalm 32:8.

4. **From His Book He gives us instruction – Luke 9:4 (And He said)**

   a) Within His Word are all the principles we need to know for ministry. Psalm 25:5.
   b) Within His Word is encouragement for our souls. Isa. 40:31; Joshua 1:9.

c) Within His Word is guidance and leading for our preaching/teaching ministry. Psalm 16:7a.
d) The Holy Spirit will be our Teacher as we seek to teach others. John 14:26.

5. On our part there must be communication – Luke 9:10 (They told)

a) This involves intimate communion with the Father in prayer. Rom. 12:12; Phil. 4:6-7.
b) Talking to God about our blessings & burdens; our ups and downs; our failures and successes in ministry.

6. He encourages us to restoration – Luke 9:10 (He took them aside privately)

a) The "rest stops" in ministry are vital to survival. Mark 6:31
b) If not careful, the work of the ministry can be debilitating – like a candle that becomes spent while it shines!

The Pastor's Portrait in the Old Testament
Isaiah 61:1-3

1. The pastor's provision in ministry – Isaiah 61:1a

a) The Spirit's presence.
b) The Lord's anointing.

2. The pastor's priorities in ministry – Isaiah 61:1b-3a

a) To preach good tidings.
b) To bind up the brokenhearted.
c) To proclaim liberty to the captive.
d) To proclaim grace and wrath.
e) To comfort all that mourn.

3. **The pastor's purpose in ministry** – Isaiah 61:3b

    a) That God's people might be called trees of righteousness.
    b) That God might be glorified.

The Pastor's Portrait in the New Testament
John 1:6-8; II Timothy 4:1-2

1. **His character** – He is a man – John 1:6a.

2. **His calling** – He is a minister – John 1:6b; Eph. 3:7.

3. **His commission** – He is a messenger – John 1:7-8.

4. **His charge** – He has a mandate – II Timothy 4:1-2.

    a) Where do faithful ministers stand? II Tim. 4:1.

    b) What do faithful ministers do? II Tim. 4:2.

    c) How do faithful ministers preach? II Tim. 4:2.

5. **His commitment** – he has a motive – I Tim. 1:18.

    a) His Commitment to God – I Tim. 1:12.

    b) His commitment to Jesus Christ – John 3:30.

    c) His commitment to the Holy Spirit – I Cor. 6:18-19.

    d) His commitment to edify the Lord's people; to evangelize the lost – I Thess. 5:11; Matt. 28:19-20.

    e) His commitment to a holy life and prayer – I Pet. 1:14-16; I Thess. 5:17.

f) His commitment to a disciplined daily schedule: personal time; study and preaching/teaching; administration, visitation and counseling – Eph. 4:12-13.

The Pastor and His Prayer Life

➤ *"Christ went more willingly to the cross than we go to the throne of grace!"* –Thomas Watson

➤ *"Prayer will make a man cease from sin, or sin will entice a man to cease from prayer. When thou prayest, rather let thy heart be without words, than thy words without heart!!"* –John Bunyan

➤ *"God never denied that soul anything that went as far as heaven to ask it."* –John Trapp

➤ *"Prayer that is faithless is fruitless."* –Thomas Watson

What Really Is Prayer?

P = **is Prevailing!** In Gen. 32:28 the angel said to Jacob, *"As a prince hast thou power with God and with men, and hast prevailed."* What does prevailing mean? It means to become effective, to succeed, to triumph.

R = **is Requesting!** Matt. 7:7: *"Ask, and it shall be given unto you."* Some pray only when trouble comes. We must pray often, asking largely.

Thou art coming to a king, large petitions with thee bring;
For His grace and power are such, none can ever ask too much! –John Newton

A = **is Accepting!** Mt. 21:22: *"Whatsoever ye ask in prayer, believing, ye shall receive."* We must ask with expectancy....and we will receive with joy and appreciation.

Y = **is Yielding!** Lk 22:42: *"...not my will, but thine be done."* Jesus was facing the cross, His life was at stake, but He yielded to His Father's will. Prayers will be answered; burdens lifted; broken homes mended; souls saved....when we yield our will to His will.

E = **is Evangelizing!** James 5:16: *"The effectual fervent prayer of a righteous man avails much."* Just think, our prayers can reach around the world to touch missionaries and loved ones. Distance is no barrier to the effects of prayer. If you don't pray for lost friends and family members, who will?

R = Rejoicing! Jn. 16:24: *"Ask and ye shall receive, that your joy may be full."* Rejoicing comes with the anticipation of knowing God can answer. Prayer is not "Now I lay me down to sleep!" It is work!

Why Do We Pray?

1. To have fellowship with God - Psalm 63:1, 5-8.
2. To know God's leading - James 1:5.
3. To be kept from evil - II Thessalonians 3:1-3.

When Can We Pray?

1. Anytime - Psalm 55:16-17.
2. All the time - I Thessalonians 5:17.
3. A quiet time - Matthew 6:6.

How Do We Pray?

1. Believing - Matt. 21:22; James 1:6.
2. Boldly - Eph. 3:12; Hebrews 4:16.
3. In the Spirit - Eph. 6:18a; Jude 20b.
4. In the name of Christ - John 16:23, 26.
5. Expecting answers - Mark 11:24; I John 5:14-15.
6. With praise & thanksgiving - Psa. 34:1; Phil. 4:6; I Thess. 5:18.

What Are Some Hindrances To Prayer

1. Unconfessed sin - Psalm 66:18.
2. Refusal to hear and obey - Proverbs 28:9.
3. A life occupied with idols - Ezekiel 14:3; I John 5:21.

4. Unforgiving spirit - Mark 11:25-26.
5. Lack of faith - James 1:6-7.
6. Selfishness - James 4:3.
7. Disharmony in the home - I Peter 3:1-7.

A Suggested Format for Establishing a Prayer Period

A. Keep seven (7) sheets, one for each day, in a notebook. Divide among the seven (7) days, things you want to pray for such as unsaved relatives and friends, church ministries & leaders, SS teachers and workers, missionaries, local, state, national leaders, and your own personal needs.

B. Day:_____ Order for prayer: Praise, confession, thanksgiving, supplication

C. <u>Specific Request</u>   <u>Date Began</u>   <u>Date Answered</u>

Concluding Thoughts

1. A pastor must prevail in prayer! A pastor must bring his requests often before the Throne Room. A pastor must ask with expectancy! A pastor must yield to the Father's will in prayer.

2. The **nine acts** of prayer: *Call unto God, adore, confess, petition, plead and then declare I am the Lord's, give thanks and bless, and let "amen" confirm my prayer.* –Isaac Watts

3. The **I.O.U.'s** of Prayer –John Piper

   Incline my heart to Your testimonies (Your Word). Psalm 119:36

   Open my eyes that I may see wondrous things from Your Word. I am a stranger in the earth; do not hide Your Word from me. Psalm 119:18

Unite my heart to fear Your Name. Teach me Your way, O Lord, I will walk in Your truth. Psalm 86:11

Satisfy us early with Your mercy, that we may rejoice and be glad all our days. Psalm 90:14

The Pastor as Servant Leader

Introduction

I love Thy kingdom, Lord, the house of Thine abode,
The church our blest Redeemer saved, with His own precious blood.

I love Thy church, O God, her walls before Thee stand,
Dear as the apple of Thine eye, and graven on Thy hand.

For her my tears shall fall, for her my prayers ascend,
To her my cares and toils be giv'n, till toils and cares shall end.
–Timothy Dwight (1752-1817)

➤ *Servant Leaders* are in ministry! It is important in ministry to understand that ministry is not something that we do for God as much as something that God does in and through us – *"For it is God who works in you both to will and to do of his good pleasure."* **Phil. 2:13**

➤ *"Ministry takes place when divine resources meet human needs through loving channels to the glory of God."* -Warren Wiersbe

➤ This definition would consider the servant-leader a common denominator through which God provides His divine resources to meet human needs.

➤ In the Bible angels have several responsibilities, one of which is being a ministering spirit. In a sense we are *"earth angels"* for we too are called to minister to others.

➤ Based on Wiersbe's definition of ministry we are *earth angels* that have a four-fold objective:

✓ We are *providentially dependent* (divine resources).

✓ We are *purpose driven* (the glory of God).

✓ We are *people* *directed* (human needs).

✓ We are *personal* *distributors* (loving channels).

Servant Leaders Are Providentially Dependent
(Divine Resources)

➤ There is a problem of becoming *"predominantly independent"* rather than *"providentially dependent"* as a Servant Leader. **John 3:30**: *"He must increase, but I must decrease."*

➤ **TRUST** believes that God CAN! (Attitude).
FAITH believes that God WILL! (Action).
PRAYER is what moves us from TRUST to FAITH...from knowing to showing... from ATTITUDE to ACTION!

"WHEN GOD WANTS A JOB DONE, FAITH GETS THE CONTRACT!"

Servant Leaders Are Purpose Driven
(Glory of God)

➤ **Ephesians 3:21**: *"Unto Him be glory in the Church by Christ Jesus throughout all ages, world without end."*

➤ In our personal lives and in the church how do we really glorify God?

1. By confessing Jesus as Lord - Phil. 2:9-11.
2. By confessing sin - Joshua 7:19.
3. By being strong in faith - Romans 4:20.
4. By our faithfulness - John 15:8; Phil. 1:11.
5. By our praise - Psalm 50:23.
6. By our suffering - Isaiah 24:15.
7. By prayer - John 14:13.
8. By unity - Romans 15:5-7.

9. By giving Him glory in everything we do - I Cor. 10:31; Acts 12:20-23.

➤ **Eccles. 5:16**: *"What profit has he who has labored to the wind?"*
➤ **John 17:4**: *"I have glorified You on earth. I have finished the work which you have given me to do."*

Servant Leaders Are People Directed
(Human Needs)

1. A true Servant Leader will be a member of the T.A.R.S. Team – a *"Turn-Around-Specialist."*
2. As we read through the Gospels Jesus was definitely a *"Turn-Around-Specialist."*

3. **Psalm 147** confirms that God is "people directed" and it must also be a trait of a Servant Leader.

Servant Leaders Are Personal Distributors
(Loving Channels)

1. A Servant Leader Must Have A *Thankful* Heart - **I Thess. 5:18** *"In everything give thanks..."*

    William Law: *"The greatest saint in the world is not he who prays most or fasts most; it is not he who gives alms, or is most eminent for temperance, chastity or justice. It is he who is most thankful to God, and who has a heart always ready to praise Him."*

2. A Servant Leader Must Have A *Happy* Heart -

    Psalm 144:13: *".....happy is that people, whose God is the Lord."*
    Psalm 100:2: *"Serve the Lord with gladness (happiness); come before His presence with singing."*

3. A Servant Leader Must Have A _Sensitive_ Heart - **1 Peter 3:8-9** – _8 Finally, all of you be of one mind, having compassion for one another; love as brothers, be tenderhearted, be courteous; 9not returning evil for evil or reviling for reviling, but on the contrary blessing, knowing that you were called to this, that you may inherit a blessing_

4. A Servant Leader Must Have An _Open_ Heart -

    Matt. 26:39_: "He fell on His face and prayed..."_
    Mark 1:35: _"He went out, and departed into a solitary place, and there prayed."_
    I Timothy 4:16_: "Take heed to yourself and to your doctrine."_

5. A Servant Leader Must Have A _Passionate_ Heart **-**

    David had a passion to Know God: _"As the heart pants after the water brooks, so pants my soul after you, O God."_ **Psalm 42:1**

    Paul had a passion to know Christ: _"That I may know Him, and the power of His resurrection, and the fellowship of his sufferings, being made conformable unto His death."_ **Phil. 3:10**

    Moses had a passion for lost people: _"Yet now, if thou wilt forgive their sin; and if not, blot me, I pray thee, out of Thy book which thou hast written."_ **Ex. 32:32**

    God's reaction to a non-passionate heart is very clear in **Rev. 3:15-16**: _"I know your works, that you are neither cold nor hot. I could wish you were cold or hot. 16 So then, because you are lukewarm, and neither cold nor hot, I will vomit you out of My mouth."_

6. A Servant Leader Must Have A _Clean_ Heart **-**

    Psalm 66:18 - _"If I regard iniquity in my heart the Lord will not hear."_
    Proverbs 4:23 - _"Keep your heart with all diligence, for out of it spring the issues of life."_

Conclusion:

1. *Ministry takes place when <u>divine resources</u> meet <u>human needs</u> through <u>loving channels</u> to the <u>glory of God</u>.*" –Warren Wiersbe

2. As Servant Leaders we must never forget that we are *<u>providentially dependent</u>* (divine resources); we are *<u>purpose driven</u>* (the glory of God); we are *<u>people directed</u>* (human needs); we are *<u>personal distributors</u>* (loving channels).

3. And in all of this we must have right hearts. Hearts that are *<u>thankful</u>, <u>happy</u>, <u>sensitive, open</u>, <u>passionate</u>* and *<u>clean</u>*!

> *"It is not great talents God blesses so much as great likeness to Jesus!"* -Robert Murray McCheyne

The Pastor and His Care Ministry

"Therefore take heed to yourselves and to all the flock, among which the Holy Spirit has made you overseers, to shepherd the church of God which He purchased with His own blood." **Acts 20:28**

The call to ministry is a profession but we must be careful not to become professionals. John Piper has an excellent volume regarding that entitled, *"Brothers, We Are Not Professionals!"* I cannot image a person experiencing a call into the ministry without being a "people" person. Some have tried and failed. A more stinging indictment of that is found in Ezekiel 34:2, 4, 6. Ministry is a choice to love and care for people.

Quayle in his book, *"The Pastor-Preacher,"* says that *"All human people want to be cared for by their pastor. Calling is important for it will aid your preaching."* Granted, some in the congregation will always be more loveable than others, but given time, loving by caring will conquer many a heart.

Admonitions in Caring For the Flock

1. Take notes. Unless you have a fantastic memory, keep everything on one calendar, organize, organize, organize and always keep a notepad on your person. Next to the Bible, in ministry you must have a calendar and notepad!

2. Be visible. Linger after services on Sundays and Wednesdays. Dr. Howard Sugden, while pastoring at South Baptist in Lansing, MI, not only walked the pews before the services greeting people, he often could be found in the parking lot greeting them before they even entered the church! Use these times to interact with the flock. Be sure to inquire of those who are quiet, that don't seem to need attention, or by nature avoid contact with others.

3. Be available. Remind your flock often that you are accessible in time of need, or just when they might need some time. Schedule such times into

your calendar. Be a good listener. Often you can answer many questions or meet needs by interacting during regular services or activities at church. In one of my churches, I made myself available upon occasion on Sunday afternoons and was surprised at some who showed up to express deep spiritual concerns in their lives. When numerous calls come in the midst of a busy day (phone calls, knocks on the study door, death in a family, emergency hospital calls) always remember: *interruptions are opportunities for ministry!*

4. Be an encourager. Acknowledge people who need to be recognized. Make phone calls. Send e-mails, texts or personal notes. When the church is small and it is possible, remember birthdays, anniversaries and make a note on your calendar on the first anniversary after the death of a loved one.

5. Be a visitor. Make time in your schedule for home, evangelistic, and hospital visitation. To not do so, is to be neglectful. Visits don't have to be long, should always include prayer (especially for some need that you might discern) and if appropriate, reading of Scripture. Leaving appropriate literature (Daily Bread, helpful pamphlets, gospel tracts, etc.) can often be helpful, and more times than not, will be read. Be passionate in your burden for lost souls. The devil loves to distract us from the task of rescuing the perishing!

6. Be responsive. Be sensitive to feelings, griefs, sorrows and patient with the failures, weaknesses and annoyances of others. Try not to be distracted when someone is talking to you. Give them your undivided attention. Especially give time to the children, on bended knee looking them in the eye so that they know that you are interested. And, of course, interact often with the young people and participate in their activities whenever possible.

7. Counseling. This is necessary but must not be all-consuming. Confine this to certain hours in the day. Never counsel or visit a woman alone. Don't hang a shingle on your door which reads "free counseling," for it is not free, it can steal your time. There will always be some that will monopolize your time and not listen to your advice. When you do counsel, give

homework and require church attendance for that is where the best counsel can be received – through the hearing of God's Word. Where the need for counseling takes you further than your ability to help, be aware of professional counselors who can be trusted and are supportive of the church's teaching, and who will share with you progress as permitted.

8. Respect confidentialities. Never share with others what has been shared with you. Never, even anonymously, use illustrations in your sermons of situations you may be involved with in your present church. Save those for later ministries.

9. Funerals. When death strikes your flock be with the family as soon as possible. Visit the home or hospital; your presence, sometimes without words, is what they need most. Involve the church family in bringing in food to the home. If requested, visit the funeral home with them to make arrangements. Offer suggestions for the memorial service but try to honor their requests. Plan the service; contact the social committee of the church to arrange for a post-service luncheon if it is appropriate. If possible, be with the family for prayer before visitation begins. Call within a couple of days following the service to see how the family is doing and if they have any needs. If an active member, have deacons keep in touch as they go through the grieving process.

10. Weddings. Don't become known as a "marrying-parson." Establish guidelines and boundaries. It is best to have these in writing and accepted by either leadership or congregational approval. This will prevent many problems for the pastor and the church. Seek out good material for pre-marital counseling. Confirm your convictions regarding marriage, divorce and re-marriage. Having a "wedding planner" in the church will save you hours of time.

11. Guard your heart. Take heed to yourselves first, and then the flock (Acts 20:28). Guard your quiet times. Don't make them a part of your sermon preparation. Learn to "bite your tongue!" A pastor who loses his temper in a board or church meeting can undo in five seconds the respect he has sought to achieve in many years of ministry. *"He who is slow to wrath has*

great understanding, but he who is impulsive exalts folly. A soft answer turns away wrath, but a harsh word stirs up anger." (Proverbs 14:29; 15:1).

12. Your preaching. Never forget that preaching is as important as teaching! Evangelism and a burden for the lost must never vanish from the pastor's heart. Remind your flock often of the cross and its redemptive power. Remind them of the awful rewards of sin. Evangelism and edification must find a balance in one's pulpit ministry. Never underestimate the spiritual needs of the flock. Preachers are proclaimers and teachers are instructors. Our charge is to do both with passion and clarity.

13. Finances. Stay out of the money affairs in the church other than encouraging your flock to faithfully give according to Scripture. Be careful in letting manipulating members bribe you for ulterior motives. Be an example in giving. I would discourage negotiating salary when considering a church. If God is calling you there He will meet your needs. Learning to trust God for your financial needs and that of your family may keep you on your knees, but it will also reveal your dependence upon the promises of God. God is pleased when we bring our faith to His promises!

14. Decision making. Learn not to make decisions quickly in ministry, but on the other hand, do not linger long indecisively. Identify the problem; get all the facts; line up the alternatives (advantages versus disadvantages); select the best option; and remember decisions must be based upon what's right and not who's right. Don't make decisions under stress. Don't try to anticipate everything. Don't be afraid of making a wrong decision. Once the decision is made, go on to something else.

15. Personal responses. In ministry we do things for the Lord, not men. Do not expect thank-yous! Do not expect praise. Do not seek praise. If given thanks for a sermon or some kind deed, simply express appreciation. Try to be a positive thinker and not get discouraged by circumstances. When personal attacks are made, spread them before the Lord rather than other people. If mistakes are made apologies should be given. A pastor who acknowledges his mistakes personally or publicly will grow in respect among his flock. There is not room for pride or egotism in the life of a

servant of God, only humility and an understanding that we can do *"nothing without Him; He must increase and we must decrease"* (John 15:5; 3:30). Failures can produce growth! Pastors are easy targets so keep on the move!

16. Dress decor. The pastor's personal appearance is important. In a day when "dress-down" is in, dress up is never out of vogue when serving the Lord. A pressed suit, shined shoes and a clean car should never be out of style, regardless of one's budget. Though church attire is much more casual today, the pastor should not lead the parade in setting dress trends. Though any may enter the house of God regardless of social or economic status, manner of dress or bodily décor, the pastor should instill a respect for the worship of a holy God through his own personal appearance.

17. Family. I often told my congregations upon my arrival that someday their church would have another pastor but that I would never have another family. Some suggestions: use your children sparingly as illustrations and only with permission as they get older; let others know you love your wife by complimenting her often and including her as a partner in ministry and certainly never embarrassing her; mentor your children as they grow and early on involve them even in small ways in the ministry; don't embarrass them by making them do things they are uncomfortable with – we all have different gifts; encourage them to participate in things they enjoy and support them with your attendance. Pray for God's guidance regarding family boundaries.

18. Timeouts. Some thoughts on "timeouts" in ministry. W.W. Wiersbe once said that, *"An off day isn't quite the same as a day off!"* Timeouts include making wise use of days off and vacations. T. Harwood Pattison once said, *"An annual vacation of at least four weeks should be given every minister. No minister can do twelve months work in twelve months, though he can in eleven!"* Pattison, a noted professor of pastoral theology, made that statement in 1907 because of the increasing pressures of that day for those in ministry! I wish churches would give pastors a month's vacation from the get-go, but whatever you receive, use wisely.

Regarding "timeouts," Charles Spurgeon told his students, *"It would sweep the cobwebs out of the brains of scores of our toiling ministers who are now but half alive!"* The pastor who takes more "days off," may just have fewer "off days!"

Profitable Pastoral Reading

Seldom are there books in which we agree with everything, but often we can find things that will enrich our ministries. Following are a few such books.

Allen, Jason K., *Discerning Your Call to Ministry*, Moody Publishers
Armstrong, John H., *Can Fallen Pastors Be Restored?* Moody Publishers
Chadwick, W.E., *Pastoral Teaching of Paul*, Kregel Publications
Ezell, Rick, *Strengthening the Pastor's Soul*, Kregel Publications
Gilmore, John, *Pastoral Politics, Why Ministers Resign*, AMG Publishers
Horner, David, *A Practical Guide for Life and Ministry*, Baker Books
Mayhue, Richard & Thomas, Robert, *The Master's Perspective on Pastoral Ministry*, Kregel Publishing
Marshall Colin and Payne, Tony, *The Trellis and the Vine*, Matthias Media
Piper, John, Brothers, *We Are Not Professionals*, Broadman & Holman Publishers
Preston, Gary, *Pastors in Pain, Growing in Times of Conflict*, Baker Books
Prime, Derek & Begg, Alistair, *On Being a Pastor*, Moody Publishers
Stott, John R.W., *The Preacher's Portrait*, Eerdmans
Trull, Hoe & Carter, James, *Ministerial Ethics*, Broadman & Holman Publishers
Ventura, Rob & Walker, Jeremy, *A Portrait of Paul*, Reformation Heritage Books

---

Three things make a preacher – reading, prayer and temptation.
–John Trapp

The doctrine of a minister must credit his life, and his life adorns his doctrine. –Jean Daille

Unholiness in a preacher's life will either stop his mouth from reproving, or the people's ears from receiving. –William Gurnall

The Pastor's Leadership Qualities

God Has Always Worked Through Leadership

1 Samuel 13:14 *But now your kingdom shall not continue: the LORD has sought him a man after his own heart, and the LORD has commanded him to be captain over his people, because you have not kept that which the LORD commanded you.*

Jeremiah 4:25 *I beheld, and, lo, there was no man, and all the birds of the heavens were fled.*

Jeremiah 5:1 *Run you to and fro through the streets of Jerusalem, and see now, and know, and seek in the broad places thereof, if you can find a man, if there be any that executes judgment, that seeks the truth; and I will pardon it.*

Ezekiel 22:30 *And I sought for a man among them that should make up the hedge, and stand in the gap before me for the land, that I should not destroy it: but I found none.*

Leadership Deficiency Leads to Church Deficiency

1. Absence of growth (Lost focus on Great Commission).
2. Discord (Have to resort to conflict management).
3. Pastoral burnout/brief pastorates (No one wants to serve on the Board).
4. Membership loss (People leave out of frustration).
5. Lost sense of mission (No longer salt & light in the community).

Leadership Qualities of Moses – First Spiritual Leader in the O.T. – Hebrews 11:24-29

1. **Faith (11:24)** – Faith is believing in God's promises (11:1); is always related to God's people (11:2); and is believing in God's power (11:3). It is impossible to lead without faith. Faith always comes with filling – *"And Stephen, full of faith and power, did great wonders and signs among the people"* – Acts 6:7. (Also Acts 7:55).

2. **Integrity – (11:25)** - There is no room for hypocrisy in leading the people of God. If men speak ill of you, live so that no one will believe them!

3. **Vision – (11:26)** – Vision is simply believing that God can do greater things in the future than He has done in the past AND being willing to be a part of it! Pessimistic leaders do not lead!

4. **Decisiveness – (11:27)** – Decision-making is a big part of leadership BUT our decisions are always weighed in the light of God's Word and God's will, not our own personal agenda.

5. **Obedience – (11:28)** - Always to God and His direction, first for your life and then for the life of the church. Obedience is the only thing we have to give Him (I Peter 1:2).

6. **Responsibility – (11:29)** – Moses was committed to trusting God and being responsible in his obligation to lead God's people to places they had never been before. That is what leadership does – it takes people where they have never been before, both in spiritual growth and church development.

Christ's Example of Leadership

(A.B. Bruce suggests that the total report of the gospels covers only 33-34 days in our Lord's three and a half years of ministry, and John records only eighteen days. What did He do with the rest of His time? The clear implication of the Scriptures is that He was training leaders.)

1. **The leadership of our Lord focused on individuals** - His personal conversation with Peter in John 21 is good example of that.

2. *The leadership of our Lord focused on the Scriptures* - Matt. 5:21-48: *"You have heard that it was said, but I say to you."*

3. **The leadership of our Lord focused on purpose** - He had clear cut goals for His earthly ministry, and a limited time in which to achieve them. In light of this the pastor should always ask, *"Would I do anything differently if I knew that I had only had three and a half years?"*

4. **The leadership of our Lord majored on being a servant -** He came to minister to, not to be ministered unto (Matt. 20:28). Visit Jesus in the upper room and learn (John 13).

Give Me a Man

Give me a man of God—one man whose faith is master of his mind,
And I will right all wrongs and bless the name of all mankind.

Give me a man of God—one man, whose tongue is touched with heaven's fire,
And I will flame the darkest hearts with high resolve and clean desire.

Give me a man of God—one man, one mighty prophet of the Lord,
And I will give you peace on earth, bought with a prayer and not a sword.

Give me a man of God—one man, true to the vision that he sees,
And I will build your broken shrines and bring the nations to their knees.
–George Liddell

Give me men to match my mountains, give me men to match my plains,
Men with empires in their purpose, men with eras in their brains.
–Author Unknown

The Pastor and Leadership Disciplines

Introductory Observations:

1. *The purpose of this session* is to remind the spiritual leader of his proper role and to provide motivation and ideas for administrative effectiveness in leading the local church.

2. *The cry of the church* is for spiritual leadership to guide them biblically through the maze of cultural diversity.

3. *In order to be leaders of the flock* there must be continual personal spiritual growth. God's leaders for building His church will be servants, godly examples, visionaries and commanders in chief.

4. *Five symptoms of deficient leadership* in many churches are: (1) absence of growth, (2) discord, (3) brief pastorates and burnout, (4) spectator religion, and (5) non-ministering churches. *(Leadership In Christian Ministry, James E. Means)*

5. *Church leadership must always keep the larger picture in mind:* **(1)** Christ is the Head of the church - not us - Eph. 5:23; **(2)** every facet of ministry must always glorify the Lord - I Cor. 10:31; **(3)** every believer in the church has a gift(s) that must be exposed and exercised in the Body - I Cor. 12-14; **(4)** how can our church best be salt & light in our community and around the world - Matt. 5:13-14?

6. *Scripture texts:* Proverbs 11:14; Acts 20:28; Ephesians 4:11-12; I Corinthians 12:5,8; I Peter 5:2; II Timothy 2.

Leaders Are Servants

1. Servants are slaves of Christ – Phil. 1:1; Luke 16:13.
2. Servants are slaves of righteousness – Rom. 6:16-18.
3. Servants are measured by position – Mat. 20:26-28.

4. Servants are not the owner but the owned – I Cor. 6:19-20.
5. Servants are not the proud, but the humble – Mt. 5:5.
6. Servants are not greater than their Lord – John 13:16.
7. Servants are not pleasers of men – Gal. 1:10.
8. Servants are doers of the will of God from the heart – Eph. 6:6.
9. Servants are selfless servers of others – Mat. 20:27.
10. Servants are honored for faithful service – Mat. 25:21.

"It's not about position, power, prestige, or privilege. It's all about moving down, not up: 'Whoever desires to become great among you, let him be your servant,' (Matthew 20:26). Thus Jesus taught His disciples that to climb the ladder of leadership, one must descent to the position of slave. To climb higher, I must go lower!"
Daniel L. Anderson, *Biblical Slave Leadership*

Leaders Are Godly Examples

"Nor as being lords over those entrusted to you, but being examples to the flock." I Peter 5:3

1. We lead through teaching - II Timothy 2:2.
2. We lead through enduring hardship - II Timothy 2:3-4.
3. We lead through personal integrity - II Timothy 2:5.
4. We lead through hard work - II Timothy 2:6.
5. We lead through personal accountability to God - II Timothy 2:15.
6. We lead through personal holiness - II Timothy 2:21.
7. We lead through our conduct: not quarrelsome, kind to all, able to teach, patient when wronged, gentle in correcting those in opposition - II Timothy 2:24-25.
8. We must have a *positive* relationship to the *Scriptures* for they mold us, guide us, encourage us and help us.
9. We must have a *personal* relationship to *others* - often our ministry is that of a bridge builder.
10. We must have a *private* relationship to *ourselves* - must be a person of strong discipline; accept hard work; be prepared to face adversity and suffering as well as blessing.

Leaders Are Visionaries

"My soul, wait silently for God alone, for my expectation is from Him." Psalm 62:5

1. Vision is expecting God to do greater things than He has ever done before!

2. You cannot be a visionary without *motivating* your people. *Motivation* involves stimulating people to a feeling of dissatisfaction with the status quo.

3. You must define the purpose of your church in a concise, written statement.

4. In light of your purpose, discover five greatest areas in the church that need to be improved. List them by importance. Invite the congregation to assist you through a survey.

5. Study each area separately listing ways in which to improve. All goals should be specific, measurable, attainable, related to your purpose and timely.

6. The importance of establishing goals: gives purpose to activity; unifies church family; provides direction; helps evaluate progress; keeps church innovative; glorifies God IF you are seeking HIS mind and direction.

7. Guidelines for all goal setting: Will it help the church's purpose? Is it a result of church interest? Can it be expressed clearly? Is there a person or group than can achieve it? Can its accomplishments be visualized as a reality? Is it achievable?

8. Always involve as many people as possible in the visionary planning for the church.

Leaders Are Commanders in Chief

"Remember those who rule over you (your spiritual leaders - Amplified), who have spoken the Word of God to you, whose faith follow....obey those who rule over you (your spiritual leaders - Amplified), and be submissive, for they watch out for your souls, as those who must give account. Let them do so with joy and not with grief, for that would be unprofitable for you." –Hebrews 13:7

Chairing Board/Committee Meetings

1. Give proper notification of all meetings and always encourage maximum attendance.

2. Mail/e-mail minutes of previous meeting and upcoming agenda prior to the meeting.

3. Be prepared to lead.....open with Scripture and prayer.

4. A simple agenda to follow: ***Informational Items*** (updating them on things they need to be aware of); ***Study Items*** (things you would like them to think about, possibly discuss, but no action taken); **Action** *Items* (business items that need to be voted upon - occasionally in a meeting study items may become action items). If you have various members or committees reporting, place them under the appropriate section.

5. Set timelines for your meetings and be sure to start on time - ending on time may be another story!

6. If possible, set consistent times for meetings and always announce the next meeting date at the end of the meeting.

Written Job Descriptions

1. Every position in the church, including pastoral staff, should have a written job description. Definition of responsibility is essential to good

performance. A job description encourages accountability as well as task description.

2. The best job descriptions are specific, definitive and measurable. Following is an example:

> Job Title
> Job Summary
> Responsible for What
> Accountable to Whom
> What is my term of service

The Decision Making Process

1. Decision making is often synonymous with problem solving, therefore:

> Identify the problem.
> Get all the facts.
> Line up the alternatives (Advantages/Disadvantages).
> Select the best option.
> Decisions must be based on what's right not who's right.

2. Guidelines for decision making:

> Don't make decisions under stress.
> Don't make snap decisions.
> Don't drag your feet.
> Don't try to anticipate everything.
> Don't be afraid of making a wrong decision.
> Once the decision is made, proceed to something else.

J. Oswald Sanders' Secrets Learned In a Lifetime's Ministry
(His book, *Spiritual Leadership,* Moody Press, is must reading!)

1. Treasure people who will pray for you every day.

2. Keep up your spiritual reading. Have a filing system for data read.
3. Trust the sovereignty of God in your life.
4. Be an early riser and a time miser. Use little gaps to best advantage.
5. Always have a little more than you can comfortably cope with.
6. Be willing to step out and do something for which you feel inadequate.
7. Never lose the desire to grow. On retirement, the Lord has something better.
8. Don't think of stopping.
9. Watch your attitude to failure.
10. Accept the disciplines of God. Suffering tempers us all. Hebrews 5:8
11. Don't let finance play a big part in your decisions.
12. As a pastor, limit your counseling and major on the Word of God and prayer. Keep up your study of the Word. Don't neglect the Old Testament.
13. Minister in the power of the Holy Spirit. The secret of the fullness of the Holy Spirit is a yielded life. Acts 5:32

Helpful Books on Leadership

Anderson, Daniel, *Biblical Slave Leadership, Regular Baptist Press*

Borden, Paul D., *Hit the Bullseye, Abingdon Press (Recommended by GARBC Resource Center)*

Biehl, Bob, *Increasing Your Leadership Confidence, Questar Publishers, Inc.*

Covey, Stephen R., *The 7 Habits of Highly Effective People, Simon & Schuster*

Dayton, Edward R., *Tools for Time Management, Zondervan Publishing House*

Eims, Leroy, *Be the Leader You Were Meant To Be, Victor Books*

Gangel, Kenneth O., *Competent to Lead, Moody Press*

Hendrix, Olan, *Management for the Christian Worker, Quill Publications*

Jones, Bruce, *Ministerial Leadership in a Managerial World, Tyndale*

Malphurs, Aubrey, *Developing a Vision for Ministry in the 21st Century, Baker Book House*

_____*Being Leaders, The Nature of Authentic Christian Leadership, Baker Book House*

Martin, G. & McIntosh, G., The Issachar Factor, Broadman & Holman Publishers

Maxwell, John C., Developing the Leader Within You, Nelson Publishers

_____The 21 Irrefutable Laws of Leadership, Nelson Publishers

Michael, Larry J., Spurgeon on Leadership, Kregel

Mears, James E., Leadership in Christian Ministry, Baker Book House

Moskowitz, Robert, How To Organize Your Work & Your Life, Doubleday

Marshall, Colin & Payne, Tony, The Trellis and the Vine, Matthias Media

Peter, Laurence J., The Peter Principle, Bantam Books

Poirier, Alfred, The Peace Making Pastor, Baker Books

Sande, Ken, The Peacemaker, Baker Books

Sanders, J. Oswald, Spiritual Leadership, Moody Press

Seger, Paul, CHIEF, Leadership Lessons from a Village in Africa, Sawubona Press

Swenson, Richard, Margin, NavPress

Swetland, Kenneth, Facing Messy Stuff in the Church, Kregel

Youssef, Michael, The Leadership Style of Jesus, Victor Books

The Pastor and His Ministry Schedule

Ministry Management

Activity is not always productivity! A pastor's work is never done so the pastor must carefully choose which work must be done. Considering the average church across America would hover around the one-hundred mark in attendance, there are some distinctive variables from working in a more structured environment. Most pastors are not responsible to punch a clock, do not have a "higher authority" (other than God) looking over their shoulder, are responsible to create their own schedule, and are often untrained in time management control. This may greatly impair God's work if one is not conscientious in his day-to-day responsibilities.

Dr. Charles U. Wagner[1], quotes from the time management book, *The Techniques of Getting Things Done*, by Donald A. and Eleanor C. Laird (presently this volume may be out of print but is available from used book stores online). They insightfully list the following work essentials of those who have succeeded in their respective vocations:

1. They had the habit of planning their work not only for tomorrow but also for goals in the future. They worked for a purpose; that purpose carried them through hardships and over obstacles.

2. They had the habit of working on things that counted. They avoided enticing distractions. They knew that the steam that blows the whistle does not turn the wheel. They worked with foresight.

3. They had the habit of saying no to things that would not help them produce. They kept on the main highway; off the detours.

4. They had the habit of reading books and magazines that would help in their work.

5. They kept priming their heads with ideas, facts, and inspiration.

---

[1] *The Pastor, His Life and Work*, Pages 158-160, Regular Baptist Press

6. They had the habit of doing the unpleasant job first. They did not paralyze present activity by letting past work hang over their heads.

7. They had the habit of making themselves work. They kept their effort alive.

8. They had the habit of deciding trifles quickly. They did not putter around trying to make up their minds what to do next.

9. They had the habit of starting vigorously and promptly, often early in the morning. They did not let the grass grow under their feet.

10. They had the habit of working like craftsmen. By working for quality, they got more done and received more satisfaction than if they had pushed for quantity.

11. They had the habit of using both hands, the habit of doing two things at once. They used each minute before it had disappeared forever. Doing nothing was the most annoying things in the world to them.

12. They had the habit of getting others to help them. They trained others to be extra hands, eyes, and heads for them.

13. They had the habit of working for more than money. Pride in a job well done, in accomplishment, was more rewarding to them than a big bank account.

14. They had the habit of taking on more work. They kept expanding their abilities and achievements. They caught up on work quickly, could take on more work easily. They kept out of ruts by broadening the high roads. They put pressure on themselves to do or sink.

15. They had the habit of requiring production from themselves, of not accepting their own alibis. They cracked the whip over themselves instead of feeling sorry for their lot in life.

Major Areas of Pastoral Ministry[2]

It is my personal experience that there are at least five major areas involved in a pastor's ministerial schedule: Personal time in the Word; Study time in the Word; Administration; Visitation; Counseling.

1. **Your devotional and prayer time must NEVER be neglected!** Keeping fresh in the Lord is essential to your own walk with the Lord and that of others. One thing I have learned over the years in ministry is *that servants are prone to staleness!* A dried up servant can only give dried up service! The servants most "seasoned" are the most in danger of staleness. Following are Paul's motivating forces in keeping his quiet time with God: Galatians 2:20 (past); Philippians 3:10 (present); II Corinthians 5:10 (future).

2. **Your study time must be carved out in stone!** Set aside your mornings when your mind is fresh. Start early in the week and attempt to have your messages done by Friday afternoon at the latest. Warren Wiersbe had the habit of praying through his messages point by point on Saturday evening asking God to use it for His glory and the benefit of others. Mark out a day once a month on your calendar for research, planning, gathering sermon ideas, praying for the Holy Spirit's guidance for direction in your preaching and teaching (John 14:26).

3. **Your administrative duties will be many but must not be neglected**! Next to the Bible – a calendar! Plan, organize, and follow through! Use your afternoons for administration if possible. Plan your days, week and month and put on your calendar (keep a day, week, and month-at-a-glance calendar). In listing your daily tasks put the hardest tasks first or they will never get done; along with board/committee/staff/counseling meetings, block out on your calendar your study times, family time, time for phone calls, mail processing, correspondence, etc. This time will also include a period for vision casting, goal setting, and dreaming (of what could be – when God wants a job done, faith gets the contract!). Plan your work and work your plan! Delegate where you can – "*It is better to get ten men to work*

---

[2] *Keeping Fresh as Servants of God*, Maynard H. Belt, Seminar Session

than to do the work of ten men" (D.L. Moody). Always answer calls, emails and texts within a reasonable time!

4. **Visitation is at the very heart of pastoral ministry – it keeps you in touch with people!** The Devil puts many distractions before the pastor and one is that of neglecting pastoral visitation. One great danger is spending too much time at the computer rather than being in the "field" visiting the flock! Pastoral visitation should include: new visitors, new members, inactive members, shut-ins, referrals, and those in the hospital. New visitors: inquire of them, thank them, inform them, pray with them; new members: get acquainted with them, encourage them, make known your availability to them, pray with them; inactive members: find out why, listen without interrupting, don't get defensive, resolve issues if at all possible, pray with them; shut-ins: take your time with them, listen to their stories, inform them of church happenings, inquire of any needs, leave a list of prayer requests, read Scripture (ask if they have any favorite texts if they are not able to read themselves) and pray with them; referrals: visit with if at all possible, inquire of their spiritual condition, follow-up on if interested, assure them of your prayers, ask if they mind if you read them a Scripture and pray with them; hospitalized: visit as soon as you hear, pray with them before surgery, follow-up after surgery but don't make your visits too lengthy, do not sit on their bed, don't talk about yourself or your illnesses, be a willing listener, see if church might assist with meals, prepare the Scriptures you will read ahead of time and make appropriate brief comments, pray with them (Matthew 25:36; James 1:27). In case of death: visit the home as soon as possible, offer to go to funeral home to plan arrangements if needed, plan the memorial service with them, make contacts with those requested to participate in the service, care for family luncheon if requested, select hymns and Scriptures, use the deceased's Bible if possible (often you can learn much from a person's Bible), prepare for a graveside service, contact the family after a few days and do what you can to help them through their grief process (minister's manuals are available to help with weddings, funerals, etc.).

5. **Counseling will be necessary but it is not your primary pastoral responsibility.** Don't hang a "Free Counseling" shingle on your office door. Try to confine your counseling to your church family if at all

possible. Find a program for pre-marital counseling.[3] In marriage counseling or any type of counseling never find yourself alone with a woman. Have your wife with you; if you have a secretary, leave office door open or have a window in your door. In any kind of counseling have homework for them to do, and if they do not do it, discontinue counseling. Encourage a certain number of church services to attend, for the best counseling may be received from consistently hearing the Word of God preached or taught. Be cautious not to become personally involved. Sometimes it may be necessary to involve the deacons for church family problems. Locate qualified Christian counselors in your area that you may refer those to who may have more deed-seeded problems than you can handle. Recognize that in personal counseling, you will "win" some; you will "lose" some. Stay true to the Word of God.

The Moral of Ministry

One's pastoral ministry involves at least five major areas which easily could require 50-70 hours per week (study, prayer, calling, counseling, administration). If you give only 20 percent of your time to each area, 80 percent will remain unfinished! The schedule will always be full. You must establish a disciplined daily schedule in order to accommodate these various aspects of shepherding the flock. You can't do it alone, but you can with the strength that God will give (Philippians 4:13; I Timothy 1:12).

"The labors of the ministry are fitly compared to the toil of men in harvest, to the labors of a woman in travail and to the agonies of soldiers in the extremity of a battle." –**John Flavel**

---

[3] *From This Day Forward – Preparing Couples for the Journey of a Lifetime* (Both the Counselor's and Couples editions are available through www.bcpusa.org and click on publications/Baptist Church Planters Store)

The Pastor's Accountability - Am I Doing the Job?

"I charge you therefore before God and the Lord Jesus Christ, who will judge the living and the dead at His appearing and His kingdom: Preach the Word! Be ready in season and out of season. Convince, rebuke, exhort, with all longsuffering and teaching." II Timothy 4:1-2

My Personal Accountability before God and the Lord Jesus Christ

1. Does my day begin, continue and end in the presence of God? Psalm 5:3; 25:5; 4:8.

2. How well does my spiritual walk line up with the eight spiritual principles found in the Beatitudes? Matthew 5:3-11.

3. Do I have a "protection plan" for the devil's fiery darts and subtle temptations? Ephesians 6:1-10; I Peter 5:6-8; II Cor. 2:11.

4. Have I learned to major on my strengths and work on my weaknesses? Proverbs 18:16; Phil. 4:13.

5. Have I learned to minister where I am planted? Acts 18:9-11; Phil. 4:11.

My Ministry Accountability before God and the Lord Jesus Christ

1. How well fed and spiritually strong is each member of my flock? Acts 20:28; I Peter 5:2a.

2. How well indoctrinated in Bible truth is each member of my flock? II Tim. 2:2; 4:2; I Tim. 4:3.

3. What efforts am I making to heal those who are spiritually ill? Ezekiel 34:2-4.

4. To what extent do I exhaust all efforts to restore backsliders? Ezekiel 34:4.

5.   To what extent do I search for lost sheep outside my flock? I Cor. 9:19-23; James 5:20.

6.   To what extent do I intercede for my flock by name? John 10:14; Col. 1:3-10; II Tim. 2:19.

7.   How well do I know my flock and their needs? John 10:3-5.

8.   With what intensity do I, as shepherd, keep assertive members of my flock from discouraging or discriminating against more passive members? Titus 2:15; III John 9; II Tim. 4:14

9.   As a shepherd am I faithful in warning of spiritual and doctrinal danger? I Tim. 4:2-5.

10.   As a shepherd do I have a reputation of scattering the flock? Jeremiah 12:10; 23:1-2.

Unholiness in a preacher's life will either stop his mouth from reproving, or the people's ears from receiving. – William Gurnall

The Pastor's personal and ministry accountability before God and the Lord Jesus Christ is a solemn responsibility - we must not take it lightly!

The Pastor and His Preaching

Introduction:

1. Regarding the study for the preaching of God's Word:

   Think of it carefully, study it prayerfully,
   Deep in thy heart let its oracles dwell.
   Ponder its mystery, slight not its history,
   None can e'er love it too fondly or well.

   The Bible the Word of God is never out-of-date,
   Its timeless mid the stress of life, His love communicates.
   Its power is all I need today, its promises all I claim.
   In all this quickly-changing world, God's Word remains the same.

2. Thomas Watson: *"It was by the ear, by our first parents listening to the serpent, that we lost paradise; and it is by the ear, by hearing of the Word, that we get to heaven. "Hear, and your souls shall live""* (Isaiah 55:3).

3. Augustine: *"The cross is the pulpit from which Jesus Christ preached of God's love for the world."* Look for the Cross when you preach from the Psalms and the Old Testament.

4. *"Over the years in my preaching I have sought to combine fact and feeling. Phillips Brooks stated that preaching is presenting biblical truth through personality and that I have tried to do."* MHB

5. J. I. Packer: *"We need more 'homecoming preaching,' preaching that hits home!"*

6. Kevin DeYoung: *"The conclusion of our teaching and preaching should emphasize more what God has done for us than what we need to do for Him."*

7. John Flavel: *"A hot iron, though blunt, will pierce sooner than a cold one, though sharper."*

8. Calvin Miller: *"When the preacher says, 'Thus saith the Lord,' they ought to let God do the talking! Preaching was established by Jesus because God has a job to do. To get the job done preaching must be committed to two goals: first, it should be passionate and second, fascinating. Preaching is rescue work, rescuing that which was lost in Genesis 3."*

9. Joseph Seaborn Jr.: *"Passion can never be genuine unless the preacher owns a burning need for a God-relationship. Zeal must own the herald before the herald can preach it into others. I believe that preachers who have no God-hunger may have some good things to say but they lack the passion that is essential to create the kingdom of God and transform the world."*

10. Calvin Miller: *"But the truth is the gospel was never just an 'ear' event. The best preachers throughout the centuries always preached highly visual, image-driven sermons."*

11. Richard Baxter: *"I preached as never sure to preach again and as a dying man to dying men!"*

Principles in Preaching

1. **Participants in Preaching**
   a) God: *"Whoever speaks let him speak, as it were, the utterances of God."* I Peter 4:11
   b) The Listener: Just because they are there does not mean they are listening!
   c) The Preacher: We must be careful of preaching unfelt truth!

2. **Practice of Prayer**
   a) For conviction and cleansing of your personal life.
   b) For counseling so that you might know upon what you should preach.
   c) For concentration during your study time.
   d) For communication for preaching is sending and receiving.
   e) For concern and compassion for there is nothing like "soul to soul" to stir the heart.

3. **The Primacy of Planning**
    a) Coordination of messages: morning, evening, Sunday school, mid-week, other.
    b) Consideration of subjects, themes, relevant topics; will they be expositional, topical, doctrinal, etc. Create a "garden" file of ideas.
    c) Cultivation is vital – allowing time for the text and subject to "grow."
    d) Christocentric in your preaching and teaching but privilege the text.

4. **Particulars of Preparation**
    a) Text selection – allow time to seek the Lord's mind.
    b) Finding the main idea of the text – read it several times.
    c) Outline text with the main idea in mind. Glean what you can by your own personal reflection upon the text, then go to the commentaries.
    d) Absorbing the truth of the text must become a part of you before it will become a part of others.
    e) Illustrations are windows for people to see in – this assists in holding their attention and understanding. You don't want a house with all windows, but a few are necessary.
    f) A good introduction grabs their attention while the conclusion should grab their heart.
    g) Application is essential. The entire message, from the title to closing prayer, must meet them where they live. Don't bore people with the Bible!
    h) Manuscript your message, that is, write it out! It is work but a discipline well worth the effort, for you as well as heartfelt communication to the people.
    i) Publicizing a series or study ahead can create interest. Don't neglect listing your sermon titles – don't keep your sermons a secret!

5. **Precautions in Preaching**
    a) Be enthusiastic! George Whitefield said, *"Speak everything as if it were your last!"*
    b) Be interesting! Listeners often have heads and minds that are closed tighter than a drum. You must get to the heart!
    c) Be authoritative! Preach in the power of the Holy Spirit and with conviction.
    d) Be specific! Be sure your message has a theme and stay with it.

e) Be Sensitive! While preaching the Holy Spirit may well bring things to mind you have not thought of before, just the things someone might need to hear.

The Supremacy of God in Preaching

The following are excerpts from John Piper's excellent book entitled, *"The Supremacy of God in Preaching."* In Chapter 3 he lists five steps in seeking to preach not in our own strength but in the strength that God supplies. In Chapter 7 he addresses the preaching of Jonathan Edwards and lists 10 characteristics of Edwards' preaching. I have summarized the statements and pasted them in the flyleaf of my Bible as reminders of both my need for God in my preaching as well as guidelines in the preparation of sermons.

Preparatory Steps to Preaching

1. **Admit to the Lord my utter helplessness without Him.** *"I am the vine, you are the branches. He who abides in Me, and I in him, bears much fruit; for without Me you can do nothing."* John 15:5

2. **Pray for help.** *"Call upon Me in the day of trouble; I will deliver you, and you shall glorify me."* Psalm 50:15

3. **Trust in a special promise.** *"Trust in the LORD with all your heart, and lean not on your own understanding; in all your ways acknowledge Him, and He shall direct your paths."* Proverbs 3:5-6

4. **Act in the Confidence that God will fulfill His Word.** *"For as the rain comes down, and the snow from heaven, and do not return there, but water the earth, and make it bring forth and bud, that it may give seed to the sower and bread to the eater, so shall My word be that goes forth from My mouth; It shall not return to Me void, but it shall prosper in the thing for which I sent it."* Isaiah 55:10-11

5. **Thank God both before and after the message.** *"Enter into His gates with thanksgiving, and into His courts with praise. Be thankful to Him, and bless His name."* Psalm 100:4

---

10 Characteristics of Jonathan Edwards' Preaching

1. **Stir up holy affections.** Hatred for sin, delight in God, hope in His promise, gratitude for His mercy, desire for holiness, tender compassion.

2. **Enlighten the mind.** Explain the doctrines, unravel the difficulties.

3. **Saturate with Scripture.** Quote the text. Show people where your ideas are coming from. Keep the Scriptures between you and the people.

4. **Employ analogies and images.** The heart is most powerfully touched when it is filled with vivid images of amazing reality.

5. **Use threat and warning.** Edwards would reject the two reasons why this type of preaching is rare to the saints today. (a) Because it produces guilt and fear; (b) because it is theologically inappropriate because the saints are secure and don't need to be warned or threatened.

6. **Plead for a response.** This is not at all at odds with the divine doctrine of the sovereignty of God. Don't just state the facts and sit down – plead for a response.

7. **Probe the works of the heart.** Based upon the biblical knowledge and experience of your own heart.

8. **Yield to the Holy Spirit in prayer.** Bathe your sermon in prayer.

9. **Be broken and tenderhearted.** Our hearts must first be broken.

10. **Be intense.** Eternity is at stake with every message.

A Minister's Preaching

(Taken from the Valley of Vision, a Collection of Puritan Prayers & Meditations)

MY MASTER GOD,
I am desired to preach today, but go weak and needy to my task;
Yet I long that people might be edified with divine truth, that an honest testimony
Might be born for Thee; give me assistance in preaching and prayer,
With heart uplifted for grace and unction.
Present to my view things pertinent to my subject with fullness of matter
and clarity in thought, proper expressions, fluency, fervency, a feeling sense of the
Things I preach, and grace to apply them to men's consciences.
Keep me conscious all the while of my defects, and let me not gloat in pride over
my performance. Help me to offer a testimony for Thyself, and to leave sinners inexcusable
In neglecting Thy mercy. Give me freedom to open the sorrows of Thy people, and to set before
Them comforting considerations.
Attend with power the truth preached, and awaken
The attention of my slothful audience.
May Thy people be refreshed, melted, convicted, comforted,
And help me to use the strongest arguments drawn from Christ's incarnation and sufferings
That men might be made holy.
I, myself, need Thy support, comfort, strength, holiness, that I might
Be a pure channel of Thy grace and be able to do something for Thee.
Give me then refreshment among Thy people, and help me not to treat excellent matter
In a defective way, or bear a broken testimony to so worthy a Redeemer, or be
Harsh in treating of Christ's death, its design and end, from lack of warmth and fervency.
And keep me in tune with Thee as I do this work.

Recommended Books on Preaching

The following books are a chosen selection of my personal library on preaching. Some of the authors have been dead a long time! Others are living but no longer are on the present scene of teaching and tutoring. Still others are more contemporary. I have learned from them all. It is vital for a preacher to not only read books on preaching but also read sermons by great preachers. Reading a sermon by faithful servants of God (or listening to a sermon on an I-Pod) before you preach a sermon can be very inspirational. Some of these volumes may be out of print or possibly reprinted under a different title or by a different publisher. Browse the book store often for good books on preaching, both used and new. Google those that interest you for the best prices and availability. The reading of such books will aid you, inspire you, humble you and bewilder you why God would call you into the company of the likes of Abraham, Moses, Elijah, Elisha, Jonah, Jeremiah, Isaiah, Paul, Peter, John, Augustine, Luther, Watson, Spurgeon, Moody and a relatively small number of others, most of whom are unnamed, compared to the large number of all mankind. –MHB

The Supremacy of Preaching, John Piper, Baker Book House
Between Two Worlds, John R.W. Stott, Eerdmans
Preaching and Preachers, D. Martyn Lloyd-Jones, Zondervan
Lectures To My Students, C.H. Spurgeon, Marshall, Morgan & Scott
The Minister as Shepherd, Charles Jefferson, Living Books For All
Expository Preaching, Harold T. Bryson, Broadman & Holman
Preaching to a Shifting Culture, Various Authors, Baker Book House
Preaching with Power, Dynamic Insights from 20 Top Pastors, Baker Books
The Approach to Preaching, William E. Sangster, Baker Book House
The Joy of Preaching, Phillips Brooks, Kregel Publishers
Famine in the Land, Steven J. Lawson, Moody Publishers
Preaching, G. Campbell Morgan, Marshall, Morgan & Scott
Selected Readings in Preaching, Al Fasol, Baker Book House
The Big Idea of Biblical Preaching, Wilhite & Gibson, Baker Book House
Biblical Preaching, Haddon W. Robinson, Baker Book House
Making a Difference in Preaching, Haddon W. Robinson, Baker Book House
Preaching & Teaching With Imagination, Warren W. Wiersbe, Victor Books
Privilege the Text!, Abraham Kuruvilla, Moody Publishers
Handbook of Contemporary Preaching, Michael Duduit, Broadman & Holman
Preaching, The Art of Narrative Exposition, Calvin Miller, Baker Book House
Exegetical Fallacies, D.A. Carson, Baker Book House
Treasury of the World's Great Sermons, Warren W. Wiersbe, Kregel Publications
Well-Driven Nails, The Power of Finding Your Own Voice, Byron Forrest Yawn, Ambassador International

The Pastor and His Preaching Calendar

Some Important Questions We Need to Ask Ourselves in Developing a Preaching Calendar

1. Where have I been in my preaching to my present congregation?

2. What do I have in the "hopper" now that I am working on and is it relevant or simply "something" I came up with?

3. How many times a week do I have to preach, teach, and talk?

4. When I am selecting sermon series and topics, what are my underlying motives and how do I come to those conclusions?

5. Will I include special days and occasions in my preaching calendar? On preaching to the occasion, Dr. D. Martyn Lloyd-Jones said, *"I believe in using almost any special occasion as an opportunity for preaching the gospel!"*

6. When I open the Bible to study the Scriptures do I come expectantly, with open mind, open ears and open heart? Do I seek it like silver and search for it as hidden treasures, in order to understand and find the knowledge of God? Proverbs 2:4-5

7. What is my primary preaching style? Expositional? Topical? Series? It will make a difference on how you prepare, how much material you need to have on hand, where you will find ideas, etc. It is good to use different styles for different times, needs, specials events, etc.

   a) Study the styles of successful preachers by listening to them or reading their works.

   b) W.A. Criswell: *"One day in Dallas I started preaching at Genesis 1:1 and seventeen years and eight months later I arrived at the last verse of Revelation!"*

c) D.M. Lloyd-Jones: *"Preach the Bible, and if you do, you will have more texts to expound than opportunities to preach."*

d) Bernard of Claivaux (1091-1153) – Once preached 86 sermons on just the first two chapters of the Song of Solomon (way to many)! W. A. Criswell 82 sermons from the Book of Revelation; D.M. Lloyd-Jones 60 messages from the Sermon on the Mount.

8. Most of us aren't "equipped" for this type of preaching but we do need to ask ourselves, *"When I leave my church what do I want to have taught my people?"*

Necessary Practice in Developing a Preaching Calendar

1. **Prayer -** *"Give yourself to prayer, and get your texts, your thoughts, your words from God."* R.M. McCheyne

2. **Place -** Find a place where you can quietly get alone with God and your thoughts with no or limited interruptions for specific periods of time; your study, quiet room at home, a friend's cottage, camp guest room, motel, etc.

3. **Period** – Set specific times for planning and put on your calendar: study breaks, down times such as holidays, late evenings, early mornings, one hour every day, one morning, afternoon or evening every week, a full "quiet" day every month (this method changed John Stott's entire ministry), one week every year, a certain number of hours while on vacation (early before the family arises).

4. **People** – How well do you know your people? We must preach to all ages and groups: children, teens, widows, singles, couples, seniors, divorcees, handicapped, the lonely, abused, those suffering, etc. Prepare your messages with "people" in mind!

5. **Planning** – if you are in it for the long haul plan your preaching/teaching far in advance, always leaving room for flexibility. Acquire folders for

Sunday school, morning and evening service, midweek, Bible Studies, etc., and constantly be inserting into these folders references, articles, illustrations, related texts, personal experiences, Etc. Being ready to study is half the battle!

The Importance of Having a "Preaching Garden"

1. **Organize a notebook** with dividers, or folders if you prefer, and label for New Years, Valentine's Day, Good Friday, Easter, Mother's Day, Father's Day, Memorial Day, July 4th, Labor Day, Thanksgiving, Christmas, funerals, weddings, family, Children's Day, graduation, missions, stewardship, prophecy, communion, doctrines, parables, miracles, great chapters, favorite verses, character studies, names of God, Etc. Your notes and ideas may well someday "grow" into sermons.

2. **Keep a note pad always handy!** NEVER be without a note pad nearby. If looking for them, ideas will come from everywhere: newspapers, book browsing, needs of people, visiting, hearing sermons, hot topics on the world scene, and often many come when awakened for some reason in the middle of the night!

3. **Establish regular "think" times!** From the seeds that you have planted in your preaching garden, "think" about what your people might need to hear; "think" about books you might need to add to your library to assist you. Use your preaching garden as a catalyst for your pulpit ministry. The discipline of just "thinking" is an art that must be mastered!

4. **Developing a Preaching Calendar that Will Accommodate and Benefit Your Congregation**

   a) **Why have a preaching calendar?** It directs your selection of themes; it offers a balanced spiritual diet for your people; it assists in your sermon preparation; it helps in keeping the interest of your congregation; people "think" in terms of seasons throughout the year and also major events taking place in "life."

b) **Always keep in mind** where you have been and where you desire to go in your teaching and preaching. Seek a balance between the Old and New Testaments, the Gospels and the Epistles, the Psalms and the Prophets, Doctrinal and Character Studies, Parables and Miracles, Book studies and Chapter studies, etc.

c) **Some various formats** for your consideration in developing an annual preaching calendar. If you preach expositional sermons through the books of the Bible, you will still want to take occasional breaks for summer series when some are away, current world catastrophes (9/11), missionary emphasis, etc.

A Basic Format
January – Easter
Easter – May or June
June-August
September-November
December

W.W. Wiersbe
Labor day to Thanksgiving
Advent Season
New Year's to Ash Wednesday
Lenten Season
Easter to Pentecost
Sumer Ministry

John R.W. Stott
Builds around three major Christian Festivals
Oct-Dec – Lengthened Advent Season
(Preaches from Creation to Incarnation/O.T.)
January to May/Easter
(The Gospels/Life of Christ)
June-Sept/Sundays after Pentecost
(The Acts, Epistles, Revelation)

Following this calendar allows you to reveal the story of biblical revelation from the O.T. of creation & prophecies of Christ to His birth, the life, miracles & parables of Christ in the N.T., and application of all these events to the believer in the Acts, Epistles and Revelation.

Monthly Calendar with Themes
January – Stewardship
February – Great Men/Love Series
March – The Church
April – Resurrection
May – New Life in Christ
June – Romance/Marriage/family
July/August – Summer Series
September – Commitment
October - Missions
November – Thanksgiving
December – Advent
(*Promote your theme with a banner and chorus of the month*)

Final Thoughts

1. Always plan your preaching series before announcing it.

2. Promote and package your preaching series.

3. Your Sunday evening and midweek studies are just as important and need as much promotion, otherwise you give the impression that they aren't as meaningful and helpful.

4. Carefully catalog all messages ever preached or taught, lest your congregation catch you in repetition.

5. Preserve your preaching in organized notebooks for handy reference.

6. Keep the "planning sheet" of your annual preaching in a visible location.

7. A couple of contrasting and closing quotes regarding the pastor and ministry!

"A man is as lazy as he dares to be!" –**Emerson**

"I read myself full, think myself clear,
pray myself hot, and then let myself go!"
–**A Spirit filled Man**

The Pastor and Ministerial Transitions
The Ethics of the Thing!

The church was here before we came, and it will be here after we go! We must always put self, pride and personal vendettas and agendas aside and always ask what will be best for the church and community. When difficult times come, or when a decision whether to leave or stay must be made, someone has to take the higher road. That one should be the pastor, the spiritual leader of the flock.[4]

How Can I Know When It Is Time To Leave A Ministry?
"The doctrine of a minister must credit his life, and his life must adorn his doctrine." –Jean Daille

1. **Valid reasons for leaving – (no brainers)**
   a) Moral or ethical failure.
   b) Doctrinal difference.
   c) Unruly family.
   d) Calling of a confidence vote.
   e) Continual decline in attendance.
   f) Pulpit voice no longer fresh.

2. **Invalid reasons for leaving – (the Devil's devices)**
   a) When you are tired and discouraged (maybe you just need a little time away).
   b) When you aren't getting your way (maybe you are being tested).
   c) When you just feel unappreciated (maybe you need to be humbled).
   d) When the work becomes difficult (maybe God is trying to stretch you).
   e) When the pay is poor (maybe God wants you to trust Him more).
   f) When the work schedule becomes unreasonable (maybe you need to delegate).
   g) When known problems become greater than you expected (no problem is greater than God).

---

[4] *The Pastor and Ministerial Transitions*, Maynard H. Belt - Seminar

3. **Feasible reasons for leaving – (only if your heart is right)**
   a) A persistent restless spirit (the Lord is shifting your burden).
   b) Complacency on part of church and/or pastor (have been together too long).
   c) A definite direction, accompanied by peace, a positive call to another place.
   d) Unresolved church conflict (years of sin not dealt with).
   e) Continued inadequate compensation (you have tried but ends not being met).

4. **The evaluation process – (soul-searching questions)**
   a) What are your primary reasons for leaving?
   b) What are the obstacles – are they permanent or temporary?
   c) Have you accomplished your goals?
   d) Have you lost your vision for the work, and if so, why?
   e) Can your spiritual gifts advance the church from where it is today?
   f) Are your philosophies of ministry still compatible?
   g) Do you still have credibility with the leadership and your church?
   h) Never rule out the Holy Spirit's working in your life and that of the church.

What Do I Do When I Am Ready To Move But There Is No Place To Go?

"There are three things in providence: God's foreknowing, God's determining, and God's directing all things to their periods and events." -Thomas Watson

1. Pray without ceasing – be sure there is no known sin in your life hindering your prayers.
2. Study the Scriptures personally – wait on the Word for some word from the Word.
3. Patiently wait until the Lord definitely leads – don't jump into something just because.
4. Share your heart and concerns with a trusted peer who will pray with and for you.
5. Work as though you are staying forever.
6. Don't let your preaching tell on you.
7. Prepare a resume and share it very sparingly and carefully.

8. Always remember that God knows both the desires of your heart and your address.

How Do I Leave When Conflict Is The Cause And I Am the Cause Of The Conflict?

"While conflict within the church does not always indicate that Satan is active, it is clear evidence that the Holy Spirit is absent." –Ron Susek

1. **What to do if you ever experience termination**
   a) Examine your life for sin.
   b) Don't allow bitterness to control your life – it's a poison that will eat away your heart.
   c) Remember that vengeance belongs to the Lord, not you.
   d) Read the Psalms constantly and apply the balm of Gilead to your soul.
   e) Keep an open communication with your wife and children.
   f) Accept the counsel of colleagues.
   g) Work on keeping a positive attitude before family and friends – Phil. 4:8.
   h) Cling to a Sovereign God who is too good to be unkind and too wise to make mistakes.
   i) Determine that you will practice what you have always preached about such times as these.
   j) Wait patiently no matter how long it takes for another door to open.
   k) Ask the Lord to help you forgive those who have hurt you.
   l) If at all possible, leave so that you can return someday without a negative reaction.

2. **How to prevent a possible termination of ministry**
   a) Be forthright and honest about your weaknesses before you go.
   b) Plan regular evaluation times with the leadership.
   c) Deal quickly and openly with any problem as soon as it surfaces.
   d) Advise your leadership to encourage people with complaints to air them biblically.
   e) Teach your leadership and church the importance of fervent prayer one for another.
   f) Guard your tongue, be careful about relationships, be a man of integrity, no hidden agendas.
   g) Keep freshness in your preaching and teaching ministry.

h) Admit your mistakes when you might be the one to blame – humility vs. humiliation.

i) Keep open lines of communication among the congregation – it's their church too.

The Pastor in Transition

"The word <u>work</u> forbids loitering and the word <u>ministry</u> lording." –John Boys

1. **Before you accept there are some important questions to ask.**
   a) Is this a realistic opportunity?
   b) Am I reasonably prepared to meet the challenge?
   c) What is the counsel of godly men whom I respect?
   d) What is the leading of the Holy Spirit?
   e) Are my wife and children open to and even excited about the transition?

2. **After you get there, here are some helpful suggestions to consider.**
   a) Let the congregation see where you live – have an open house.
   b) During the first year get acquainted, build trust and listen; then make it a habit!
   c) Unless necessary, let changes wait for a little while – some people don't like sudden change.
   d) Make yourself known in the neighborhood and community.
   e) Develop your vision for the future – contemplate how to make it the church's vision also.
   f) Make your deacon's meetings a time of spiritual refreshment as well as business.
   g) Never demean the former pastors – if they loved them, they will love you too.

3. **While you are there, always keep the big picture in mind.** *"Ministry takes place when divine resources meet human needs through loving channels to the glory of God."* –Warren Wiersbe
   a) We are providentially dependent (divine resources).
   b) We are purpose driven (glory of God).
   c) We are people directed (human needs).
   d) We are personal distributors (loving channels).

Things You Should Never forget If You Are Genuinely Called to Ministry!

As His servants, His chosen pastors, we have been given the greatest privilege and responsibility in all the world – we are called to be ministers of the living God, called by the Sovereign Lord, to do His will in fulfilling His eternal plan. Let's finish well, and finish faithful, for His honor and for His glory! – MHB

1. You are chosen by God Himself – Isaiah 43:10; Jeremiah 1:5-7.
2. You are chosen by Jesus Christ – John 15:16; I Timothy 1:12.
3. You are chosen by the Holy Spirit – Acts 20:28.
4. You are counted trustworthy by Jesus Christ – I Timothy 1:12.
5. You have been called to be a minister by the gift of God's grace – Ephesians 3:7.

Some helpful Books for Pastoral Ministry

Bratcher, Ed (Kemper, Scott) *Mastering Transitions*, Multnomah

Haugk, Kenneth C., *Antagonists in the Church (How to Identify & Deal with Destructive Conflict)*, Augsburg Books

Shelley, Marshall, *Well-Intentioned Dragons (Ministering to Problem People in the Church)*, Word Books

Susek, Ron, *Firestorm, Preventing & Overcoming Church Conflict*, Baker Books (A Must!)

Thomas, Curtis C., *Practical Wisdom for Pastors*, Crossway Books

Wiersbe, Warren W., *On Being a Servant of God*, Baker Books (A Must!)

Lessons Learned in Laboring for the Lord
(Practical insights from a Pastor's itinerant journey down Ministry Lane)

1. **Always be able to back up your sermon points with Scripture**! There may be some in the congregation who know more than you!

2. **If we will take care of the spiritual, God will take care of the financial**!

    a. He will take care of the _church_ if they are obedient.

    b. He will take care of the _pastor_ if he will simply trust - Phil 4:11-12 *"Not that I speak in regard to need, for I have learned in whatever state I am, to be content: 12 I know how to be abased, and I know how to abound. Everywhere and in all things I have learned both to be full and to be hungry, both to abound and to suffer need. Phil 4:19 And my God shall supply all your need according to His riches in glory by Christ Jesus."*

3. **Whenever God wants a job done, faith gets the contract!** In Matthew 9:27-31 Jesus said to the two blind men who wished to be healed, *"...be it unto you according to your faith."*

    a. There are at least 10 different levels of faith in Scripture and it is important that we keep moving up the ladder: _No faith_ – Mk. 4:36-40; _Little faith_ - Matt. 14:25-31; _Weak faith_ - Rom. 14:1; _Dead faith_ - James 2:17; _Vain faith_ - I Cor. 15:14; _Great faith_ - Lk. 7:9; _Rich faith_ - James 2:5; _Unfeigned faith_ - I Tim. 1:5; _Precious faith_ - 2 Pet. 1:1; _Holy faith_ - Jude 20.

    b. If you do what you have always done – you will be what you already are!

4. **When it comes to conflict in the church between the pastor and leadership, or the pastor and the congregation – someone has to be bigger!** God calls the pastor to be the *"spiritual"* leader in all kinds of circumstances and there should always be evidence of the fruit of the Spirit in his life.

    a. Should a pastor have to leave, no change of circumstances can repair a defeat of character (Horace Greeley).

b. Sometimes life's choices are made for us, and when they are, God is no less in control than if we had made them ourselves.

c. We only learn to value God when we come to know Him by experience. Never be afraid to leave an unknowing future to an all-knowing God. - Isa. 24:15

d. You can never be like the Lord Jesus if you have never been wounded or hurt by those you love.

e. *As soon as we cease to bleed - we cease to bless.* -John Henry Jowett

5. **When you have a good idea, plant it in the hearts of a few good people and be patient while it grows**. Someday, they will say, *"Hey! Let's do this...,"* and it may be your idea.

6. **Be sure to follow through on what you say, or be prepared to pay the consequences.** We must be people of our word. Learn to write things down so that you don't forget!

7. **The response to your messages may be in proportion to the time you spent in preparation of them.** *"If preaching is an act of worship, then the preacher must not present to God that which costs him nothing!"* Statement by Wiersbe in his book, *Real Worship!* Oliver Nelson Publishers.

> *2 Sam 24:24: Then the king said to Araunah, "No, but I will surely buy it from you for a price; nor will I offer burnt offerings to the LORD my God with that which costs me nothing." So David bought the threshing floor and the oxen for fifty shekels of silver."*

8. **In John Piper's paperback, _The Supremacy of God in Preaching_ (Baker), he lists 10 characteristics of Jonathon Edwards's preaching that are helpful reminders before going into the pulpit** (mentioned in *"The Pastor and His Preaching"*): *Stir up holy affections; Enlighten the mind; Saturate with Scripture; Employ analogies and images; Use threat and warning; Plead for a*

response; Probe the workings of the heart; Yield to the Holy Spirit in prayer; Be broken and tenderhearted; Be intense.

9. **When you can't teach old dogs new tricks - find new dogs!** The longer some people have done things one particular way, the more difficult it is to get them to change. Sometimes you just have to get some new people saved (or maybe the old ones saved!) and teach (disciple) them from scratch. One of our primary objectives should be to ignite *fresh faith.*

10. **Purity of life in the pastorate is an absolute essential.** When temptation knocks on my door I keep these reminders before me: *I remember my conversion; I remember my call; I remember my clan (family); I remember my congregation; I remember He's coming!*

11. **If I really want to know what God is thinking, I must read and study the Bible!** If we really want to help our people know what God is thinking, we must help them read and study the Bible!

    a. *"We read the Bible to know God!"* -W. Wiersbe

    b. *"I will never be the man of God I ought to be if I'm ignorant of the Word of God."* -Wilbur Rooke

12. **In ministry, it is extremely important to praise and encourage your people.** A pat on the back and a kick in the seat are only eighteen inches apart but there is a world of difference in their meaning! Learn to be a grateful pastor.

13. **I have never liked interruptions *in* ministry, but I have learned that interruptions are often opportunities given by the Lord *for* ministry.** Our Lord's ministry was one of constant interruptions - but also providential opportunities to fulfill the purpose of His call.

14. **Work diligently in not being addicted to activity but dedicated to results!** It is possible to have myriads of ministries taking place, but nothing being accomplished. Establishing tangible goals is essential.

a. Asking my flock to assist me in setting tangible goals that they can help accomplish has also been extremely productive.

b. Early in ministry I "ran" the show. Then one day, while lying in a hospital bed I learned that others could "run" the show and do it quite well.

15. **Do not sacrifice the foundation of the permanent for the desire of the immediate.** *"It takes 100 years for an oak tree to develop and 100 days for a squash; which do you want to be?"*

16. **Psalm 118:24 and Psalm 34:19** have become important verses of Scripture to help keep me focused in my day-to-day ministry for the Lord. What verses do you have?

> *Ps 118:24 This is the day the LORD has made; We will rejoice and be glad in it.*
> *Ps 34:19 Many are the afflictions of the righteous, But the LORD delivers him out of them all.*

17. **I thank God for the many great "friends in ministry" He has brought into my life over the years.** You can never have too many of them! Through being encouraged *by* others I have learned to be an encourager *to* others. There are "friends" and then there are "friends!"

a. *"Friendship is one of the sweetest joys of life. Many might have failed beneath the bitterness of their trial had they not found a friend."* -Spurgeon

b. *"Five years from now you will be pretty much the same as you are today except for two things: the books you read and the people you get close to."* -Charlie "Tremendous" Jones

18. **I must keep on keeping on for there are those coming behind me that need what I know!** Dr. Franklin Logsdon once told me that Dr. William L. Pettingill, on his deathbed in 1949 said to him, *"In the last days there will not be a dearth of preaching the gospel, but of practicing the gospel."* Another godly servant said, *"It is not what pastors teach, but what they tolerate, and what they tolerate is worldliness."*

Psalm 71:18 Now also when I am old and gray headed, O God, forsake me not; until I have shewed thy strength unto this generation, and thy power to everyone that is to come.

19. I Shall Not Pass This Way Again

I shall not pass this way again, Lord, help me not to stray.
Take me by Your loving hand, please guide me all the way.

I shall not pass this way again, Lord, encourage me as I go.
May I enjoy the good and bad, that from Your hand may flow.

I shall not pass this way again, Lord, may I a blessing be.
Where'er I go, what'er I say, may it always glorify Thee. MHB

20. Books that have impacted my life as I travel down Ministry Lane.

My Utmost for His Highest, Oswald Chambers
Spiritual Leadership, Oswald J. Smith
Valley of Vision, A Collection of Puritan Prayers & Devotions, Bennett
Between Two Worlds, The Art of Preaching in the 20th Century, John Stott
Preaching and Preachers, D. Martyn Lloyd-Jones
Lectures to My Students, Charles Spurgeon
On Being a Servant of God, Warren Wiersbe
Walking with the Giants; Talking with the Giants; Combined in a new
    Volume entitled, *Living with the Giants,* Warren Wiersbe
Warning to the Churches, J.C. Ryle
All Things for Good (Romans 8:28), Thomas Watson
Christ Is All, Horatius Bonar
Memoir and Remains of R.M. M'Cheyne, Andrew Bonar
Awake My Heart, J. Sidlow Baxter
The Complete Works of E.M.Bounds on Prayer, Baker Books

CPSIA information can be obtained
at www.ICGtesting.com
Printed in the USA
LVHW061457041218
599229LV00012B/522/P